T0083808

Confucius Institutes

Confucius Institutes:
Academic Malware

Marshall Sahlins

PRICKLY PARADIGM PRESS
CHICAGO

© 2015 Marshall Sahlins.
All rights reserved.

Prickly Paradigm Press, LLC
5629 South University Avenue
Chicago, IL 60637

www.prickly-paradigm.com

ISBN: 9780984201082
LCCN: 2014949662

Printed in the United States of America on acid-free paper.

> The Confucius Institute is an appealing brand for extending our culture abroad. It has made an important contribution toward improving our soft power. The "Confucius" brand has a natural attractiveness. Using the excuse of teaching Chinese language, everything looks reasonable and logical.

So runs the report of a speech in November 2011 by Li Changchun, then a member of the Standing Committee of the Politburo, the highest body of the Chinese Communist Party, at the Beijing Headquarters of the Confucius Institute. Officially known as The Office of the Chinese Language Council International and commonly as "Hanban," the Confucius Institute is a Chinese government agency inserted into an increasing number of universities and lower schools the world around, ostensibly with the reasonable and logical mission of teaching Chinese language and culture–and veritably with the practical mission of promoting the real-political influence of the People's Republic.

Since their inception in 2004, Confucius Institutes (CIs) have been a great success. Presently there are approximately 450 Confucius Institutes operating in 120 countries, including about 100 in the US, and some 650 "Confucius Classrooms" offering instruction in K-12 schools. Among the American host institutions are the prestigious private universities of Chicago, Stanford, and Columbia and the exemplary state universities of Michigan, Iowa, and UCLA. The entire public school district of Chicago has enlisted in the program, putting 43 Confucius Classrooms in primary and secondary schools with an enrollment of nearly 12,000 students. An obvious reason for this success is the great demand for Chinese language instruction the world over, which in turn suggests a "follow the money" meme, as the demand clearly reflects the global prowess and glowing promise of the Chinese economy.

Less obviously, Confucius Institutes are often hostages to university fortunes, insofar as they are deemed desirable and renewable at the risk of jeopardizing the flow of tuition-paying students from China. Totaling more than 235,000 in 2013-14, these students comprised the largest national contingent of foreign enrollees in American colleges and universities. Still following the money, one should not ignore the various perquisites provided by Hanban to this or that host institution: ranging from tours to China for students in CI courses; to funding research on China by graduate students and faculty (pending approval of the project by Hanban); to wining and dining of university presidents and their families on visits to China, featuring first class air travel, five star hotels, and celebrity tourism—an up-to-date version of the imperial guest ritual of the T'ang dynasty.

Moreover, there is the immediate payoff for the universities concerned: $100,000 and up in start-up costs provided by Hanban, with annual payments of the like over a five-year period, and instruction subsidized as well, including the air fares and salaries of the teachers provided from China. After a period of training by Hanban, the Chinese teachers are in many cases integrated in the university's degree programs, in charge of regular credit courses. Hanban also agrees to send textbooks, videos, and other classroom materials for these courses—materials that are often welcome in institutions without an important China studies program of their own. In other words, American universities and others are subcontracting teaching to a foreign government.

The teaching component of the local Confucius Institute is often complemented by academic programs such as guest lectures and scholarly conferences on China. Considering that the political constraints in effect on public discussions of certain topics in China are usually followed in Confucius Institutes—no talking of Tibetan independence, the status of Taiwan, the fourth of June 1989 at Tiananmen Square, Falun Gong, universal human rights, etc.—these academic events are largely consistent with the "cultural activities" of CIs, insofar as they likewise present a positive picture of a peaceful, harmonious, and attractive People's Republic. From classes on making dumplings to film showings, celebrations of Chinese festivals, and "traditional" folk dances, the CIs put on various "culturetainments" (as Lionel M. Jensen dubbed them) for the community at large. According to the *Constitution and By Laws of Confucius Institutes*, the annual plans of local CIs must be submitted to Beijing for approval, and Hanban reserves the right to take any CI to court for sponsoring an event it has not first approved.

But none of this has ever happened, say a chorus of Confucius Institute Directors. Hanban has never told us what to do or not to do, they say. No plans of CI events, no research proposals have ever been turned down by Beijing. And most telling, it is claimed that despite the great number of CIs the world around, there have been very few incidents of academic malpractice. Perhaps so when the matter is a public scandal, but something is to be said for what is considered a violation of academic integrity, and what therefore passes for an "incident."

What usually passes for an incident of this kind is the oft-cited charge of discriminatory hiring against McMaster University in 2012 by an erstwhile Confucius Institute teacher from China, Ms Sonia Zhao, who was unable to maintain her position when she revealed her adherence to Falun Gong. Brought before the Human Rights Tribunal of Ontario, the incident did become a scandal to the extent that McMaster was moved to terminate its Confucius Institute. Yet there are numerous similar events of similar implication that, because they are too parochial or seemingly insignificant, never reach public attention. Indeed, when the "incident" consists of self-censorship on the part of a secondary school teacher in a Confucius Classroom in Ashtabula with regard to topics that are politically taboo in China, the matter is not likely to come to anyone's attention. Nor would it be necessary to go so far as preventing the Dalai Lama from speaking on campus to make an offense of that nature against academic freedom. I am told on good authority that while it is perfectly possible to hang a portrait of the Dalai Lama in the Center for East Asian Studies at the University of Chicago, it would be impossible in the Confucius Institute. The quotient of iconicity (ikonicity) in the image is enough to make the point—even though *ceci n'est pas un Dalai Lama*.

Incidents of academic malpractice in Confucius Institutes, from the virtually unnoticeable to the publicly notorious, are in fact disturbingly common. In what follows I describe a good number of them, based on reports in public media and communications from persons in the institutions involved. A prefatory notice of the views of Chinese officialdom on the politics of culture and Confucius Institutes, together with some reference to the shadow governance of Hanban by the CCP apparatus, will help make these incidents intelligible.

But before going any further, I should make clear the reasons for my temerity in thus entering a debate about Confucius Institutes. This pamphlet has everything to do with the challenges CIs pose to academic freedom and integrity in the US and elsewhere; and although it is necessarily concerned with Chinese government policy, it nothing to do with animus to the PRC as such, the Chinese people, or with some sort of deranged anti-communism. Then, there is the reticence of China scholars with ongoing research interests in China to become engaged in criticism of the CI project. Regrettably, it becomes necessary for people like me to take up these essentially domestic, US issues of academic integrity.

Official Chinese Views on the Politics of Culture and Confucius Institutes

Make sure that all cultural battlegrounds, cultural products, and cultural activities reflect and conform to the socialist core values and requirement.

—Liu Yunshan, Minister of Propaganda,
7 September 2010, *People's Daily*:
(http://culture.people.com.cn/GB/22226/
57597/57600/12691228.html)

Coordinate the efforts of overseas and domestic propaganda, further create a favorable international environment for us. Overseas propaganda should be "comprehensive, multi-level and wide-ranging."... We should do well in providing services and exercising control and management of foreign journalists; we should guide them to report China objectively and friendly. With regard to key issues that influence our sovereignty and safety, we should actively carry out international propaganda battles against issues such as Tibet, Xinjiang, Taiwan, Human Rights, and Falun Gong. Our strategy is to proactively take our culture abroad... We should do well in establishing and operating overseas cultural centers and Confucius Institutes.

—Liu Yunshan, Minister of Propaganda,
January 2010, *Yongning Government Website*:
(http://yongning.gov.cn/ynkxfzg/contents/
265/2221_5.html)

Take the year 2010 as an example, we sent 940 art and cultural groups to perform in foreign countries, totaling 93,700 performances... Compared to 2009, the number of performances in foreign countries increased by 25.4 percent. If we organize government-sponsored activities, foreigners might be on high alert... Many of our cultural products have an intense ideological overtone... The Confucius Institute is semi-official... It will be useful to expand China's influence abroad.

—Xu Shipi, a scholar close to officialdom, March 2012, *China.com*: (http://opinion.china.com.cn/ opinion_20_35820.html)

Amidst the ever more frequent confrontation and blending of different ideas and cultures worldwide, whoever occupies the highest point of cultural development will have in possession strong cultural soft power, and will be a proactive player in the intense international competition... The hostile forces in the international community are hastening their steps to westernize and separate our country. The ideology and culture fronts have been their key areas of infiltration. We must deeply understand the seriousness and complexity of ideological struggles, and take powerful measures to cope with them.

—Hu Jintao, CCP General Secretary, 1 January 2012, *China.com*: (http://www.china.com.cn/ policy/txt/2012-01/02/content_24306776.html)

Every year since 2004, Li Changchun gave numerous important instructions to the Confucius Institute and visited Confucius Institutes in 15 countries when traveling abroad. He has established a favorable image as a Chinese leader in the international society. The series of important instructions by Li Changchun on the Confucius Institute are theoretical treasures of the Confucius Institute undertaking. We studied them in the past, and we must continue to study them now and in the future.

—Xu Lin, Director of Hanban (Headquarters of the Confucius Institutes), November 2011, *Confucius Institute Online*:

(http://edu.chinese.cn/onlinelearning/Notes/
NotesDetail.aspx?AnnouncementID=79)
(excerpt from the report on Li Changchun's visit,
cited above)

The international spreading of culture must shoulder the tasks of improving our nation's soft power and creating a better image... The cross-media spreading model for our culture has not only increased our influence internationally, but also broadened our strategic interests... We should quietly plant the seeds of our ideology in foreign countries, we must make good use of our traditional culture to package our socialist ideology.

—Wang Gengnian, Director of China Radio
International, 2011, *People's Daily*:
(http://theory.people.com.cn/GB/
16480463.html)

Culture is one important component of our nation's soft power. It plays an important role in strengthening our nation's comprehensive power, and thus has an influence on the overall development of our Party and the country.

—Jia Qinglin, member of the CCP Politburo
Standing Committee and Chairman of the National
Political Consultative Conference, 24 July 2007,
163 News: (http://news.163.com/07/0725/09/
3K84OOV0000122EH.html)

The Confucius Institute opened up a new channel for China's foreign relations. It has made significant contributions to improve China's soft power.

—Special Topic Conference of National Political
Consultative Conference, 26 August 2011,
China News: (http://www.chinanews.com/cul/
2011/09-15/3330742.shtml)

We require from you, Chinese residents, staff at Chinese enterprises, faculty of Confucius Institutes, and Chinese students in Kirghizstan, that no matter what work you do in a foreign country, keep China's peaceful unification in your mind.

—Association for China's Peaceful Unification, Kyrgyzstan, 25 January 2012, *State Council Website*: (http://www.gwytb.gov.cn/gatsw/fdct/201202/ t20120214_2291723.htm)

Note the presence of members of the Standing Committee of the Politburo, the supreme ruling body at once of the Communist Party and the State, among those giving guidance to Confucius Institutes. This is some contrast to the way Hanban commonly identifies itself—and is commonly known abroad—as a "non-profit organization affiliated with the Ministry of Education." Some such benign description can be found on the website of virtually every university Confucius Institute, thus giving it a semblance of academic legitimacy. Indeed in more elaborate formulations the CI adds a certain moral authority in describing itself as "an independent, non-profit organization affiliated with the Ministry of Education devoted to fostering instruction in Chinese language and culture in the aim of promoting a harmonious multicultural world order." What is generally not said either in Beijing, Ann Arbor, or Palo Alto is that Hanban itself is ruled by a "Governing Council" of high Party-State officials—although both the make up of that Council as specified in the *Constitution and Bylaws of Confucius Institutes* and its actual membership can be found on Hanban websites (http://english.hanban.org/node_7880.htm) (http://www.chinese.cn/conference11/node_37099. htm).

However, what cannot be publically found, at least not easily, is the shadow Party organization that sits above Hanban and its Governing Council, setting its policies, funding its operations, and otherwise supervising it. Hanban functions within and as part of the Chinese Communist Party's Propaganda and Education system. Until recently the propaganda czar in charge of the system was Vice-Premier Li Changchun—the one who said in a speech at the Confucius Institutes Headquarters that "using the excuse of teaching Chinese language, everything looks reasonable and logical."

The Governing Council of high officials is the bureaucratic body that controls Hanban. Its own chair, Madam Liu Yandong, is a Vice Premier of State and member of the Politburo. Under Madam Liu are four Vice-Chairs: the Ministers of Education and Overseas Chinese Affairs, the Deputy Secretary General of the State Council, and the Vice Minister of Finance. A third tier of Executive Council Members includes Vice Ministers of Foreign Affairs, National Development and Reform, Education, Commerce, Culture, State Council Information, and Overseas Chinese Affairs, among others. Occupying a relatively modest place in the hierarchy as the thirteenth and last mentioned of these Executive Council Members is Vice Minister Xu Lin, the Director General of Hanban (its CEO, in effect). There is a fourth tier of ordinary "Members," including a decorative collection of foreign Directors of university CIs. The Governing Council, Madam Liu Yandong and the higher officials in charge, controls the annual agenda and receives the reports of the Hanban Headquarters in Beijing—even as the Headquarters receives and approves the annual reports of Confucius Institutes in schools the world over. It follows that in submitting these reports of their Confucius Institutes to the Beijing Headquarters, Stanford, Columbia, Chicago et al put themselves in the position of dependent peripheral branches of a bureaucratic network whose policies come down from the higher reaches of the Chinese Party-State.

Moreover, these policies come rather from the Party than the State. For through its own ranking Party members, the Governing Council of Hanban is in turn subject to the Chinese Communist Party Propaganda system. As is well known, the CCP is "the state of the state," although exactly what this entails is not well known, because the Party tends to conceal the extent and manner of its influence.

As investigated by David Shambaugh in 2007 and Stephen J. Hoare-Vance in 2009, the imbrication of the Confucius Institutes in the CCP apparatus consists primarily in the membership of ranking members of the Hanban Governing Council in the so-called "Small Leading Groups" of the overarching Propaganda and Education system. Consisting of eight or so Party (cum State) officials, the important Leading Groups are headed by a member of the Politburo Standing Committee. It is through their participation in a Leading Group that these officials convey CCP policies into the functioning of the bureaucracies in which they hold important positions. As of last notice, Party policies are transmitted to the Confucius Institutes largely by virtue of the double appurtenance of officials of the Hanban Governing Council in the External Propaganda Leading Group or the Propaganda and Thought Work Leading Group. The mission of the External Propaganda Leading Group, according to Shambaugh, is:

(1) to tell China's story to the world, publicize Chinese government policies, and promote Chinese culture abroad; (2) to counter what is perceived to be hostile foreign propaganda (such as the so-called "China Threat" Theory); (3) countering Taiwan independence proclivities; and (4) propagating China's foreign policy.

Such are the kinds of policies to which members of the Hanban bureaucracy are beholden and for which they are accountable (David Shambaugh, 2007, "China's Propaganda System: Institutions, Processes and Efficacy," *The China Journal* 57: 25-58, see pp.48-49; see also Stephen T. Hoare-Vance, 2009, "The Confucius Institutes and China's Evolving Foreign Policy ," M.A. Thesis, University of Canterbury, NZ [http://ir.canterbury.ac.nz/bitstream/10092/3619/1/Thesis_fulltext.pdf]).

It follows that the Confucius Institutes are not simple non-profit organizations affiliated with the Ministry of Education and devoted to promoting a harmonious multicultural world. Indeed, although host CIs are told they are funded by the Ministry of Education, the MOE is just a laundering front for the CCP's External Propaganda Group. Shambaugh writes:

Another prominent example of external propaganda work is the substantial effort to establish a range of "Confucius Institutes" around the world…. [F]oreign universities are typically approached by the Education Counselor of the local Chinese embassy offering "no strings attached" funds to establish a Confucius Institute. The recipient is told that the funding comes from the Ministry of Education, but it is in fact laundered through the MOE from the

CCPPD's External Propaganda Department [CCPPD = Chinese Communist Party's Propaganda Department].

Analogously and more generally, the Confucius Institutes implement policy directives of the Party. Consider the encomium accorded by Xu Lin, the Director of Hanban, to Li Changchun, the Head of the CCP's Propaganda and Education network, as cited above: "The series of important instructions by Li Changchun on the Confucius Institute," said Madam Xu, "are theoretical treasures of the Confucius Institute undertaking. We studied them in the past, and we must continue to study them now and in the future." In sum, Hanban takes its marching orders from the Party's propaganda apparatus—as issued from the Standing Committee of the Politburo.

This being the organization and functions of the Confucius Institutes, the comparison too often made to institutions such as the British Council or the Goethe Institut is, dare one say, a red herring. Not only are the CIs unlike these other cultural exports by their existence within and as elements of host universities, they are also distinct for functioning there as elements of a foreign government. Hence the contradictions to academic norms exemplified in the following pages.

Censorship in University Activities:
Self- and Other

—A scheduled 2009 visit of the Dalai Lama was cancelled by the interim Chancellor of North Carolina State University, Jim Woodward, ostensibly because there had been insufficient time to prepare for such an august guest. The director of the NC State Confucius Institute, Bailian Li, a forestry professor, got involved—after the cancellation, he said, as a warning for the future—telling the provost that a visit by the Dalai Lama could disrupt "some strong relationships we were developing with China." In this connection, the provost, Warwick Arden, observed that a Confucius Institute presents an "opportunity for subtle pressure and conflict." (*Bloomberg.com*: 1 November 2011: http://www.bloomberg.com/news/2011-11-01/china-says-no-talking-tibet-as-confucius-funds-u-s-universities.html)

—In April 2013, Sydney University officials cancelled a scheduled June visit of the Dalai Lama and required it be moved off campus and show no sign of the University's affiliation. It was widely reported, including statements of Australian politicians, that the University wished to avoid "damaging its ties to China, including funding for its Confucius Institute." (*The Guardian*: 18 April 2013). Bowing to a large protest, the University administration eventually reversed itself, and the Dalai Lama spoke on campus as scheduled.

—The previous August the Confucius Institute at Sydney had sponsored a lecture by a Chinese academic known for criticizing the Dalai Lama as the leading proponent of the ancient "feudal serfdom system;" whereas China, which "had always governed Tibet," had under the PRC regime finally delivered it from "a dictatorship of monks and aristocrats." The CI, however, asked the professor to concentrate his remarks on the history of Tibetan Buddhism and the traditional, pre-Chinese selection of the Dalai Lama (*theaustralian.com*: 13 Aug 2012).

—According to Ted Foss, the Deputy Director of the Center for East Asian Studies (CEAS), University of Chicago, a picture of the Dalai Lama could be hung in the CEAS, but not in the precincts of the University's Confucius Institute (CIUC) (*The Nation*: 13 Nov 2013).

—Between July and October 2013 at Fudan, Nankai and Xiamen universities, Hanban sponsored a series of workshops for foreign directors of Confucius Institutes—over 200 directors from 188 CIs. A generally sympathetic report on the Fudan workshop published by the USC Center on Public Diplomacy notes that the lectures included some unprecedented topics, including "A New Outlook on Chinese Diplomacy," "How to Understand Contemporary China," and "History of Chinese Culture and Territory." "The selection of topics," observed the report,

> is interesting for at least two reasons: first, these contemporary themes are normally not often debated in Confucius Institutes...more often than not CIs don't talk too much about topics that are considered "sensitive" by Hanban and they focus more on topics that are—at least at first glance—

more apolitical. Generally speaking there is nothing wrong with this focus, although one may argue that this approach does not really help to show and introduce the "real China" to the world. Secondly the selection of topics indicates that Hanban wants to present Beijing's official point of view to its foreign directors. When asked about what he was told in the session on Chinese territory and culture, one foreign director told me that the lecture of course noted that Taiwan and Tibet are part of China.

The reporter was not concerned that this would be grist for critics of CIs because, "it is one thing to tell foreign directors that Taiwan is part of China, while it's another story to actually express this point of view." And although this happens occasionally, "more often than not CIs try to stay away from these topics and do more apolitical stuff like paper cutting." Still the reporter concludes: "what all this illustrates, however, is the fact that CIs are not apolitical organizations as some CI s are claiming."   (http://uscpublicdiplomacy.org/blog/what-foreign-confucius-institutes-directors-learn-china)

—Observes Daniel A. Bell, professor of political philosophy at Tsinghua University, Beijing, there is nothing sinister about Confucius Institutes: "Of course, if they wanted to use the money to organize a symposium on Tibetan independence they might run into trouble." (*The Diplomat*: 7 March 2011)

—Falk Hartig of the Queensland University of Technology (Brisbane) published an online version of a paper presented at the 2010 Asian Studies Association of Australia titled, "Confusion about Confucius Institutes: Soft Power or Conspiracy? A Case Study of

Confucius Institutes in Germany" (http://asaa.asn.au/ASAA2010/reviewed_papers/Hartig-Falk.pdf). The paper included reports of interviews with the directors of eight German CIs. All of them echoed the kind of statement that can be duplicated from many CI directors in the US and elsewhere, to the effect that Hanban does not tell them what to do or interfere in their activities. (They are contractually obliged to submit their annual plan of activities, including academic lectures and conferences, to Hanban for approval.) It put Hartig in mind of the old Chinese saying, "the sky is high and the emperor is far away;" in any case, as he also says, "the crucial point is not so much what is happening at Confucius Institutes [teaching is barely considered in the study] but much more what is not happening." The following are statements by Confucius Institute directors—names withheld by Hartig—about the limits of what can be discussed at CI events:

> The independence is limited regarding precarious topics. If topics like Tibet or Taiwan would be approached too critical [sic], this could be difficult. (Director A)

> Even though it is true China is now more open in the cultural sphere, the Confucius Institute staff knows "of course in which context we operate." (Director B)

> According to another study of CIs in Berlin, Hamburg, and Hanover, at the Third Confucius Institute Conference in 2008, while there were "no direct content-related precepts" it came up "that the following topics are not very welcomed: Tibet, Falun Gong and Taiwan." Hartig confirmed this statement with one of the (unnamed) directors in his study.

> Confucius Institutes are not an institute for anti-Chinese [sic] organizations, like dissident groups or Falun Gong. It would be dewy-eyed to affirm this. We know where we stand and I think we make use of the space we have. But that Falun Gong appears here, that's a physical impossibility. (Director B)

> I square it with my conscience or with what I know about China [in determining] what we can do and what we cannot do. (Director C)

Hartig explicitly refrains from a "final judgment" on self-censorship,

> but it can be argued that staff members of Confucius Institutes or members of Confucius Institute councils—mostly recognised scholars—wouldn't risk their reputations doing active propaganda for the Chinese government. But on the other hand it is also obvious they wouldn't risk losing the money coming from Hanban by covering anti-Chinese topics [sic].

—The Director of Confucius Institute, University of Chicago, Dali Yang, is not worried about propaganda [at CUIC] because: "Students taking classes offered by the Institute are unlikely to be victims of propaganda, he said. 'Is it possible that University of Chicago students are going to be brainwashed?'" (*Chicago Tribune*: 4 May 2014)

Comment: The implication is that censorship is permissible in courses taught by CI instructors because the students are too bright to be fooled by it. Would this be true of the 12,000 students of K-12 levels in the 43 Confucius Classrooms in Chicago Public Schools?

—In an interview, Ted Foss, the Deputy Director of the Center for East Asian Studies, at the University of Chicago, observed, with regard to possible discussions of Tibetan independence, the Tiananmen massacre, or Falun Gong at the Chicago Confucius Institute, "I think there is a certain amount of self censorship." Instead, he allowed, there is money for that kind of discussion at the CEAS.

Comment: This is again permissible censorship, here in a form something like being just a little bit pregnant: censorship can be permitted anywhere in the university, so long as there is somewhere it is not, where anything can be said. The same sort of statement—"you can always do elsewhere what we can't do here"—is a common refrain among CI directors.

—Dali Yang, Director of the Chicago CI, likewise dismisses concerns about censorship by saying that conferences on politically sensitive topics can be sponsored instead by the Center for East Asian Studies.

—The Dean of the School of Arts and Humanities at the University of Texas-Dallas, Dennis Krantz, when asked if he would seek Hanban funding for a conference on Tibet, said, "If I would do a conference on something like that, I have multiple places where I'd look for funding." (*Bloomberg.com*: 1 Nov 2011)

—Deputy Director of the Confucius Institute at Erlangen-Nurenberg, Michael Lackner, says, "Confucius Institutes are not necessarily the right place for debates on topics pertaining to touchy subjects like Tibet." Better to leave such subjects to Sinology departments. (*Deutsch Welte*: 25 January 2012)

—A report in *The Australian* cited several CI directors' claims of complete freedom from Hanban direction. Apparently the reporter did not ask about the politic discretion that might be observed by the directors themselves. However, Mobo Gao, the Director of the Confucius Institute at the University of Adelaide did offer

> that he would be unlikely to invite someone to his centre to give a talk about Tibetan independence. But in his opinion, such political activity would also be out of place within the scholarly context of a Chinese studies department at a university, whether or not it hosts a Confucius Institute.

(http://www.theaustralian.com.au/archive/higher-education/chinas-soft-power-play/story-fnama19w-1226178665629)

—Human rights are not discussed at the Confucius Institute of the British Columbia Institute of Technology, according to BCIT officials, because "it is not part of our mandate." (*Vancouver Sun*: 2 April 2008).

—In the Fall of 2013, Steven Levine, emeritus professor of Chinese politics and history at the University of Montana, wrote to over 200 Confucius Institute directors on behalf of an international group of China scholars and others, to ask that their Institutes mark the 25th anniversary of the Tiananmen events of 4 June 1989 with a public activity such as a lecture, a teach-in, or a round table discussion "that addresses the relevant historical and contemporary issues." The request continued: "In the Analects (2:24) Confucius himself said, 'Not to act when justice commands is cowardice.' We appeal to your conscience and sense of justice to act with courage." With the exception of one positive message, Professor Levine received no other response from his two hundred plus correspondents. (http://www.chinafile.com/Debate-Over-Confucius-Institutes#comment-496; also, http://sinosphere.blogs.nytimes.com/2014/02/18)

Comment: with the one possible exception, these Confucius Institutes found it expedient to ignore the events of 1989 at Tiananmen.

—Meiru Liu, Director of the CI at Portland State University, in response to a critical press report on Confucius Institutes, said that her Institute has sponsored lectures on Tibet

> with an emphasis on the beautiful scenery, customs and tourist interest…. We've also invited speakers to give lectures that cover such topics as China's economic development, currency, US China relations that includes topics related to China's military, environmental and sustainability relations [although she didn't say what the emphases were in these lectures]….We try not to organize and host lectures on certain issues related to Falun Gong, dissidents and 1989 Tiananmen Square protests.

For one thing, she said these are not topics the Confucius Institutes headquarters would like to see organized by the institutes. For another, "'they are not [of] major interest and concerns now by general public at large here in the US.'" (http://www.oregonlive.com/business/index.ssf/2011/03/oregon_pacific_rim_roundup_bei.htm)

—Durham University Professor Don Starr states Confucius Institutes have no ideological agenda because they don't even talk about such things as human rights. He says,

> another point undermining the notion that there's an ideological agenda at play is that the programme just doesn't touch on some key issues. The Chinese are going to avoid contentious areas such as human rights and democracies and those kind of things.

(*The Diplomat*: 7 March 2011)
Comment: duh.

—In an interview, the Deputy Director of Center for East Asian Studies at the University of Chicago, Ted Foss, said of research projects submitted by the Chicago CI to Hanban for funding, "there hasn't been any direct interference...but there is a certain amount of self censorship." However, he also said there has been a certain amount of "push back" from Hanban about research projects submitted by the CI that are not concerned with contemporary Chinese development.

—When the dean of students at Tel Aviv University closed down a student art exhibit depicting PRC oppression of Falun Gong, a District Court judge ruled the school had "violated freedom of expression" due to the dean's fear that the exhibit would jeopardize Chinese support for the University's Confucius Institute and other campus activities. The student plaintiffs were awarded court costs. (*Jerusalem Post*: 1 October 2009; *Chronicle of Higher Education*: 22 October 2010)

—A University of New South Wales academic (who wished to remain anonymous) told *Tharunka* [the UNSW student newspaper] that staff have been instructed not to speak to the media about charges of CI censorship of politically fraught issues, and that doing so might damage their careers. However,

> former diplomat and visiting Professor at the University of Sydney, Dr. Jocelyn Chey, was more forthcoming about her concerns. Chey said that while China needs to expand its program of cultural exchanges, she's worried that the Confucius Institute's funding ventures in universities damage its legitimacy. "It can prejudice the independent work of researchers...It's nothing specific about China, it's just a matter of academic independence."

The Director of the UNSW Confucius Institute responded that the only function of the CI was to promote Chinese language and culture and nothing else; but the *Tharunka* journalist pointed out that one of the CI board members was president and co-founder of the Australian Council for the Promotion of Peaceful Reunification of China and Chairman of the Oceanic Council for the Promotion of the Peaceful Reunification of China. (19 February 2012) (http://tharunka.arc.unsw.edu.au/963/)

—In a directive issued by the CCP to local party committees in May 2013, China's top propaganda offi-cials banned the discussion of seven topics on the grounds that they were "dangerous Western influ-ences," urging the local cadres to enforce the ban in universities and the media. The seven dangerous topics were: universal values, freedom of speech, civil society, civil rights, the historical errors of the Chinese

Communist Party, crony capitalism, and judicial independence. The ban was immediately protested as the "7 speak-nots" by a political scientist at East China University of Political Science and Law on his website—as several of these topics had been openly discussed in universities for years—but his post was just as quickly deleted, and thereupon the censors in effect made discussions of the "7 speak-nots" an "8th-speak-not." It not only stands to reason that these topics would be unwelcome in Confucius Institutes too, it is well nigh inevitable, since the directive was issued through the same propaganda apparatus of the CCP that controls Confucius Institutes.
(http://www.globalpost.com/dispatch/news/regions/asia-pacific/china/130529/censorship-chinese-communist-party) (http://globalvoicesonline.org/2013/05/16/chinese-government-bans-seven-speak-not-school-subjects/)

Comment: there are considerably more than 7 or 8 "speak-nots." As Perry Link writes:

> *I will not be persuaded by an objection that says the June Fourth example is an extreme, and therefore negligible, case, and that there are plenty of other things to talk about in bustling Big China. I will not be persuaded because, if we rule out not just June Fourth but all the other "sensitive" issues—Xinjiang, Tibet, Taiwan, Falun Gong, Occupy Central, the Nobel Peace Prize, the spectacular private wealth of leaders' families, the cynical arrests of rights advocates and sometimes their deaths in prisons, and more—we are left with a picture of China that is not only smaller than the whole but crucially different in nature.*

(http://www.chinafile.com/Debate-Over-Confucius-Institutes#comment-496)

Direct Chinese Political Influences

—In the 2013 version of an annual variety show staged on China Central Television to mark the Chinese Spring Festival, a Canadian opera virtuoso, Thomas Glenn, joined a Chinese opera star in a duet from an old "red opera"—whose meaning was unknown to him, as he had never been informed of it since he learned the song in 2011 in a program called "I Sing Beijing" sponsored by Hanban. "I gather CCTV got ahold of my performance through 'I Sing Beijing,'" Glenn said, "and the Confucius Institute asked me to do the performance for the [Spring Festival] Gala; it was the Confucius Institute that was the liaison." The irony is that the performance in question came from one of the Eight Model Operas promoted by Madame Mao during the Cultural Revolution that, among other functions, were used to attack Confucius himself—who was then and for long vilified by the PRC regime. Including such lyrics as "the Party gives me wisdom, gives me courage," the song tells of the infiltration of an encampment of "bandits," aka Nationalist soldiers, by a revolutionary hero leading to the final destruction of the Nationalists and their leader. The original libretto is said to have been meticulously revised by Chairman Mao. When informed of the meaning of the song and opera, Glenn allowed that put him in an awkward position. "To be perfectly honest," he said, "I'm largely ignorant of the social context in which this comes into play. Know that I have a very deep fondness for the Chinese people." *Comment: this is a rare glimpse into what can pass as "cultural" activities in Confucius Institutes.* (A video of Glenn practicing one of the songs is available on YouTube. See also:

http://www.theepochtimes.com/n2/china-news/
canadian-performs-red-opera-at-beijing-propaganda-
show-346600.html)

—In March 2011, the Association of Asian Studies—
representing some 8000 Asia scholars—refused
support from Hanban, "due to the lack of a firewall
separating China's government from funding deci-
sions." (*Bloomberg News*: 1 November 2011)

—Among the "General Principles" stated in the
Constitution and Bylaws of Confucius Institutes is the
mandatory requirement that CI language courses shall
be in Mandarin only: "The Confucius Institutes
conduct Chinese language instructions in Mandarin
using Standard Chinese Characters." What is here
misleadingly called "Standard Chinese Characters"
refers to the simplified script officially promulgated by
the Chinese government as a more easily learned alter-
native to the traditional characters in which everything
had been written for millennia—and much that is not to
the liking of the regime continues to be written in
Taiwan, Hong Kong, Malaysia, Singapore, Toronto,
and the other communities of the Chinese diaspora.
The simplified characters have made it possible to
greatly increase literacy in the People's Republic. In a
detailed critique of the politics of the mandatory
language rule for CI students, however, Michael
Churchman observes that it would create a global distri-
bution of scholars only semi-literate in Chinese,
restricted by and large to what has been printed in the
PRC. Native speakers of Chinese, knowing the relevant
context and idioms and having some exposure to traditional characters, may not have great difficulty deci-
phering the traditional characters, but not foreign

students, especially not those who learn the language at college age. Unable to read the classics except in the versions translated and interpreted in the People's Republic, cut off from the dissident and popular literature of other Chinese communities, students operating under Hanban rules, Churchman writes, cannot even the access "the large and growing corpus of material on Communist party history, infighting, and factionalism written by mainlanders but published exclusively in Hong Kong and Taiwan." He concludes: "The control through Confucius Institutes of what can and cannot be taught as Chinese is equally rooted in the control of what can and cannot be discussed in China." (http://www.chinaheritagequarterly.org/articles.php? searchterm+206_confuciud.inc&issue+206).

Commenting on Churchman's work, the *China Heritage Quarterly* editor, Geremie R. Barme, wrote: "Of course, for those educated solely in simplified characters, and therefore 'unlettered' in the grand corpus of pre-1960s Chinese literature, history and prior culture can prove to be challenging if not unreadable." More generally, Professor Jocelyn Chey of Sydney University notes that, "learning language is not just a technical skill…Language is the vehicle of culture." And of politics, in ways that might surprise: Professor Chey gives as an example the tension between the simplified characters of mainland Chinese and the old characters which others, Taiwan included, insist represent the true Chinese tradition. "'It's not simple to say you're going to teach Chinese. It's what sort of Chinese you're going to teach, what textbooks are you going to use. It's political,' she says." (http://www.theaustralian.com.au/archive/higher-education/chinas-soft-power-play/story-fnama19w-1226178665629)

—Writing in June 2014, the Sinologist and journalist Isabel Hilton noted that British universities are now heavily dependent on overseas students of whom Chinese students are a large cohort. They are welcome, she says:

> What are not welcome, and there are many examples from around the world, are attempts by Chinese officials to condition intellectual life in the host institutions—be it by discouraging a visit by the Dalai Lama or Rebiya Kadeer, or, as happened in one case, vetting the invitation list to a conference on the sage himself—through threats to discourage future Chinese students from enrolling in the university. Such cases are not answered by CI MOUs [Memoranda of Understanding], since the dependency is real.

(http://www.chinafile.com/Debate-Over-Confucius-Institutes#comment-496). Hilton also writes of her own experience with a CI:

> I contributed to a short book for 6th Formers (12th graders) on China, without knowing that it was sponsored by a CI. The chapter was to the length requested, and it was not until I saw a copy at the launch event that I discovered that an entire passage about the work and subsequent arrest of the Lake Tai campaigner Wu Lihong had been excised. I wish I could believe that it was just coincidence.

—A number of incidents of classroom censorship are reported in an ethnographic study by Jennifer Hubbert of Confucius Classrooms (nine Chinese teachers) in a secondary school on the West Coast of the US. Whenever "politically laden questions" emerged in classroom discussions, the teachers refocused on language issues or cultural activities:

Hubbert explicitly reports that Hanban teachers were trained to ignore or divert discussion of such issues (see McMaster incident below).

Hubbert tells of instances of that description concerning the status of Taiwan and Tibet. When students were assigned to write reports on Chinese provinces, those who chose Tibet were told to focus exclusively on cultural practices.

The reported interest of many students in the 1989 crackdown at Tiananmen Square was likewise frustrated by teachers' responses in anodyne cultural terms—characterized by one student as "look at the funny bunnies." *(Apparently the students had had too many pandas for answers.)* (Jennifer Hubbert, "Ambiguous States: Confucius Institutes and Chinese Soft Power in the American Classroom: In press, *Political and Legal Anthropology Review*)

—A North Carolina man whose wife is Taiwanese relates the experience of his daughter in a Confucius Classroom:

> The first day in class the teacher asked all the students with obvious Asian heritage to say where their families were from. When my daughter said her mother was from Taiwan, the teacher said, "Taiwan is part of China." Months later, during some free minutes in class, my daughter was looking at a map, which showed Taiwan and all of the South China Sea as belonging to China (naturally, since all of the teaching materials come from China). The teacher approached, bent down, and whispered in her ear: "Taiwan is part of China."

(*Facts and Details*, 2008, updated April 2012, http://factsanddetails.com/china.php?itemid=19040)

—McMaster University withdrew from the international Confucius Institutes in 2012 following a complaint of discriminatory hiring brought against the school in the Human Rights Tribunal of Ontario. The complaint was filed by a former CI teacher at the McMaster CI, Sonia Zhao, who said that the University was "giving legitimation to discrimination" because her contract forced her to hide her belief in Falun Gong. A copy of Ms Zhao's contract signed in China and obtained by *The Globe and Mail* included the provision that teachers "are not allowed to join illegal organizations such as Falun Gong"—a proscription that could have been found also on the Hanban website, but removed after the McMaster affair. In 2012, a year after coming to Canada, Ms Zhao recounted that she had hidden her adherence to Falun Gong from the Chinese authorities. In interviews connected with her case, she also revealed how the Chinese authorities hide the Falun Gong from classrooms of the Confucius Institutes.

> If my students asked me about Tibet or about other sensitive topics, I should have the right to express my opinion—I was not allowed to talk freely. During my training in Beijing they do tell us: "Don't talk about that. If the student insists, you just try to change the topic or say something the Chinese Communist Party would prefer."

Ms Zhao's case against McMaster went to mediation. Yet note the implication: a Canadian university had to take legal responsibility for promulgating the political agenda of the People's Republic of China.

Made aware by the Zhao case of the CI hiring practices—although the Falun Gong proscription had been on the Hanban website for some time—McMaster terminated its CI agreement. In explanation, the assistant vice-president of public and governmental relations said: "we have a very clear direction on building an inclusive community, respect for diversity, respect for individual views, and ability to speak about those." In an update on its website in 2013, the University noted that the Confucius Institute's hiring practice "excluded certain classes of applicants, which is not consistent with the university's values of equality and inclusivity, nor with McMaster's anti-discrimination policy." (*The Globe and Mail*: 7 February 2013; *China Digital Times*: 22 June 2012; *Times Higher Education* 4 April 2013; *The New York Times*: 17 June 2014; *Bloomberg.com*: 1 November 2011).

Comment: The McMaster case would only be a newsworthy effect of a pervasive defect in the standard agreements between Hanban and US or Canadian universities, since the agreement specifies that the laws and regulations of both China and the host country are in force. The effect is an endemic contradiction that condemns the host universities to complicity in discriminatory hiring, inasmuch as beliefs and practices deemed illegal in China and thus disqualifying otherwise competent teachers—such as membership in Falun Gong, advocacy of universal human rights or democratic reform— are protected by law in the US and Canada. More generally, consider the applicability of the Chinese law of higher education to American or Canadian academia, insofar as that law is explicitly designed to serve the Chinese Communist Party by promoting "socialist material and spiritual civilization" and upholding the ideological orthodoxy of "Marxism-Leninism, Mao Zedong Thought and Deng Xiaoping Theory." See Zhonghua renmin gongheguo jiaoyufa (Higher Education Law of the PRC) Ministry of Education of the PRC (1999). (http://www.moe.edu.cn/publicfiles/business/htmlfiles/moe/moe_619/200407/1311.html)

—Claims by officials of the Confucius Institute and the Center for East Asian Studies that the University of Chicago fully controls the hiring process of CI teachers from China turn out to be misleading. According to the Chicago faculty member in charge of engaging the Chinese teachers, Hanban recommends the candidates—whose eligibility is thereby limited by PRC laws and custom: no Falun Gong, human rights advocates, etc.—and no teachers recommended by Hanban have been rejected by the University (*The Nation*: 12 November 2013).

   Comment: by this arrangement, the University is complicit in discriminatory hiring.

—Italian parliamentarian Matteo Mecacci writes:

> In our own investigation, in 2011, the International Campaign for Tibet (while not identifying our Tibet connection) requested resource materials on Tibet from a Confucius Institute at a university in the Washington, D.C. region. Instead of scholarly materials published by credible American authors (not to speak of Tibetan writers) what we received were books and DVDs giving the Chinese narrative on Tibet published by China Intercontinental Press, which is described by a Chinese government-run website as operating "under the authority of the State Council Information Office...whose main function is to produce propaganda products."

(http://www.chinafile.com/Debate-Over-Confucius-Institutes#comment-496).

—"We don't know anything about the contract they [Hanban] force their teachers to sign," said Glenn Cartwright, Principal of Waterloo's Renison University College, which houses the Institute. "I'm sure they have some conditions, but whether we can dictate what those conditions can be is another story." (*The Globe and Mail*, 7 February 2013, "McMaster closing Confucius Institute over hiring issues," http://www.theglobeandmail.com/news/national/education/mcmaster-closing-confucius-institute-over-hiring-issues/article8372894/)

—In 2008, the academic director of the CI at Waterloo, Yan Li—a former reporter at Xinhua, the CCP's official news agency—took action to protest the local media's coverage of a Tibetan uprising and successfully mobilized her students to do the same. In an article on a North American website for Chinese literature scholars, Madam Li recounted these efforts to block local sympathy for the "Tibetan separatists." Rallying the CI students to "work together to fight with the Canadian media," she took class time to recount her version of Tibetan history and the current situation. Thereupon, the students launched a campaign against the Canadian media, protesting to newspapers, TV stations, and on the internet against coverage they claimed was biased in favor of Tibetans. The campaign succeeded to the extent that one TV station publically apologized for its presentation of the conflict.
(http://www.theepochtimes.com/n2/world/canadian-spymaster-fadden-warns-confucius-institutes-aim-to-teach-more-than-language-39243.html);

(http://yaleglobal.yale.edu/content/confucius-campus)

—The early versions of the Memorandum of Understanding—with reference to which all institutes are founded—states that the signatories accept the One-China Policy (with regard to the status of Taiwan). This clause was later removed.

> --Internal Hanban documents, secured by faculty in some institutions where applications were underway for the establishment of an institute, offer details of how CI representatives are to report to Chinese consulates and embassies. Such documents have also revealed a pattern of discriminatory hiring by Hanban of their teachers and staff.

(Lionel M Jensen, "Culture Industry, Power, and the Spectacle of China's 'Confucius Institutes,'" in *China in and beyond the Headlines*, 3rd edition, 2012. Timothy B Watson and Lionel M Jensen, eds., pp. 292-93)

—A video and a chapter in an advanced history text for Confucius Classrooms on "The War to Resist US Aggression in Korea," among other lessons, tell that China entered the war when the US bombed Chinese villages across the border. The video was originally in the children's section of the Hanban website. It was taken down in 2012 after Professor Christopher Hughes of the London School of Economics sent a link to colleagues considering CI teaching materials. Professor Jane Teufel Dreyer, after studying several such videos and the events they relate wrote: "they are outrageous distortions of what actually happened."

The sole chapter of the history text on the PRC period within China does not mention the Great Leap Forward or the Cultural Revolution. (Hanban.org; *Epoch Times*: 27 June 2012)

—In late July of this year, the Director-General of the Confucius Institutes in Beijing, Vice Minister Xu Lin, shocked the several hundred scholars attending the annual meeting of the European Association of Chinese Studies (ECAS) in Braga and Coimbra, Portugal by ordering certain pages torn out of the conference program and the volume of conference abstracts. The Confucius Institutes Head Office was a co-sponsor of the EACS conference through one of its academic projects, the Confucius China Studies Program. There is, however, an important condition attached to such Hanban grants, namely that, "The conference is regulated by the laws and decrees of both China and the host country, and will not carryout any activities which are deemed adverse to the social order." There's the rub (again), insofar as certain free-doms of speech and belief that are protected by law in European countries—let alone necessary for productive scholarly interchanges anywhere—are prohibited by government decree and deemed adverse to the social order in China.

"This was the first time in the history of the EACS that its conference materials had been censored," observed Professor Roger Greatrex of Lund University, the President of the Association. During and after the conference he publicly criticized Madam Xu's actions, affirming that such interference in the proceedings of a democratically organized academic organization is "totally unacceptable." Still, if it was a first for the EACS, it was not so for the Confucius

Institutes. Yet rarely have Confucius Institutes revealed their political aspect so manifestly as in Vice Minister Xu's meltdown in Braga.

Upon inspecting the conference documents at the time of her arrival, Madam Xu brusquely observed that the contents of certain abstracts were contrary to Chinese regulations. She also objected to parts of the conference program: particularly to the favorable self-representations of the co-sponsor, the Chiang Ching-kuo Foundation (CCKF) of Taiwan—in contrast to the lesser notices of the Confucius Institutes. Without a by-your-leave, Madam Xu forthwith commanded her entourage to remove all the conference programs and abstracts until her demands for the deletion of the offensive pages were satisfied. The documents were sequestered in the apartment of one of the Chinese teachers of the Confucius Institute at the University of Minho in Braga.

Throughout the next day, while complex nego-tiations were taking place between the CI and EACS authorities, some three hundred members of the Association registering for the meeting were unable to obtain these necessary conference instruments—or any cogent reason for their absence. When the conference materials did reappear the day after, one page had been torn out of the abstracts and three from the program. By then widespread resentment of Hanban was being expressed by conference participants. And something like consternation among attendees from China, espe-cially those who had registered early and were required by a CI official to turn in their copies of the relevant texts because of a "printing error."

It is not known exactly which abstracts Vice Minister Xu deemed contrary to Chinese laws and decrees, but apparently she was presented with a choice of substantially mutilating a 300-page volume of academic papers or withdrawing Hanban's association with it. Choosing the latter, she removed the frontispiece of the volume advertising the sponsorship of the Confucius Chinese Studies Program, cancelled Hanban's participation in the conference, and demanded that its contribution of 28,000 euros be refunded. This penalty fell on the account of Professor Sun Lam, Director of the Minho Confucius Institute, who had negotiated the grant and now was in effect fined for her errors—even as Vice Minister Xu covered her own.

The issue objectionable to the People's Republic represented in the missing pages of the program was the independent and honorable presence of Taiwan. Beside the self-description of the co-sponsor, the Chiang Ching-kuo Foundation, this included references to the book donations and book exhibit organized by the Taiwan National Central Library. Although the program had in fact been cleared in advance with Hanban, its commendation of the Taiwan contribution was for Madam Xu a potent symbolic attack on the PRC's denial of Taiwan's independence—a complaint soon enough echoed in the official Chinese press.

Under the headline, "There's No Shame in Hanban Tearing Up Overseas Conference Program," the *Global Times*, an official tabloid offshoot of the *People's Daily*, lauded Madam Xu's acts of censorship as patriotism; and on the same principle of complying with official Chinese regulations, the paper demonstrated how foreign academics working under Hanban's auspices are expected to censor themselves. The European Association of Chinese Studies, the report warned, "should not lack clarity over the gravity of the Taiwan problem for China." There should be no confusion about this, it said: "The reference to the CCK Foundation in the program should not have appeared in the first place."

Comment: the principle here is that foreign scholars funded by or associated with Hanban should not lack clarity about the Chinese politics of their academic work, and accordingly should refrain from taking positions objectionable to the PRC authorities. That is too often what does go down in Confucius Institutes.

Public opinion in China, as registered on the popular internet site *Weibo Sina*, ranged from support for Madam Xu to criticism of Confucius Institutes as a global joke—which foreigners dont get because of their cupidity. In tones of dismay and anger, one participant from the People's Republic at the EACS conference recounted her experience at length on the internet, complaining, as many of her countrymen have, of the large expenditure of money to educate foreigners while so many children of the rural poor go unschooled. "On finding out the truth about what happened," she said,

> I felt speechless and out of breath. How could the government do its work in this way...spend large sums of taxpayer money, gathered up by people saving on clothing and eating sparingly, on building up the image of the country...for a negative result, taking their ways of doing things at home with them abroad, and taking their way of intimidating people at home with them as they go abroad...

(http://www.21ccom.net/articles/dlpl/shpl/2014/0806/110647.html)

Comment: The contradictions between the Chinese government's "ways of doing things" and the laws and customs of countries hosting Confucius Institutes threaten to become all the more intractable with the advent of the "new sinology" being promoted by Hanban in the form of the Confucius China Studies Program (CCSP). Developed in the past few years with the object of extending Hanban's reach further into "core teaching and research" of participating universities, the CCSP sponsors a variety of projects on China by foreign PhD students, faculty members, and persons with BA degrees, ranging from doctoral research with joint Chinese and foreign university degrees, to international conferences and enhanced language training. To be eligible, however, one must be in an institution that has a Confucius Institute. Hanban will thus acquire direct control over acceptable research, conference speakers and topics, etc.—subject always to the proviso that the work conforms to the laws and regulations of China and is not deemed adverse to social order.

(http://english.hanban.org/node_43075.html)

Installing and Rejecting Confucius Institutes: The Conflict of the Faculties

—An article in *The Australian* spoke of the possibility that Confucius Institutes could take over established China studies departments—something that has also been attempted and sometimes has succeeded in the US (see below). In this case, a review panel at the University of Newcastle in April 2011 proposed that the Newcastle CI join the regular China faculty "until such time that the discipline is strengthened by a suitably qualified staff and that this occurs under the guidance of the Confucius Institute." In October the faculty of Education and Arts endorsed the proposal, with the proviso that the major in Chinese studies "be replaced with a minor in Chinese offered by the Confucius Institute." In a document of a month earlier obtained by the paper, the convener of the existing China studies program, Xia Li, objected that academic independence was at stake: that the university was proposing, "to transfer, in very certain terms, the principle of university autonomy with regard to the size of the [China studies] discipline, suitability of staff, qualifications of staff, research, and teaching contents and methodology to a non-academic, foreign institution." Ms Li went on to say that China's own academies and universities would not tolerate the like, citing the relocation of the Goethe Institut off the campus of the Beijing Foreign Studies University "to avoid the perception of outside dependence and interference." The takeover was also protested by students of China studies in a petition asking for "for truth, accountability (and) transparency;" as several felt betrayed at being "palmed off to an external body." Said one: "no one is

really keen about the concept except the University."
(http://tharunka.arc.unsw.edu.au/963/) The China
students were supported by the Chinese Community
Council of Australia and the Newcastle University
Students' Association. The latter noted:

> The Confucius Institute is not an academic institu-
> tion. It is a Chinese Government-run cultural insti-
> tution. Students of the Chinese major are students
> of the University of Newcastle, not the Confucius
> Institute. This puts autonomous Australian educa-
> tion in jeopardy.

(http://www.theaustralian.com.au/higher-education/
newcastle-asked-to-rethink-chinese-studies-downgrade/
story-e6frgcjx-1226185023954)

    In the upshot, Newcastle downgraded its
Chinese studies major to a minor but backed off the
takeover by the Confucius Institute. However, Ms Li
was offered redundancy as convenor of the China
program, and the CI instructors would be teaching in
the minor. Observed *The Australian*:

> The contentious nature of Confucius Institutes has
> meant that universities have taken various steps to
> reassure wary academic staff. These steps include the
> establishment of institutes outside faculty structures,
> sometimes in a building away from the main
> campus, and assurances that institutes will not have
> any influence over academic programs in Chinese
> studies.

(http://www.theaustralian.com.au/higher-education/
newcastle-to-axe-chinese-major/story-e6frgcjx-
1226195978612)

—A petition to eliminate Confucius Classrooms from the New South Wales public schools with some 10,000 signatures was tabled by the Greens in the NSW Parliament in October 2011. Jamie Parker, Greens MP from Balmain, explained:

> The NSW government has admitted that topics sensitive to the Chinese government, including Taiwan, Tibet, Falun Gong, and human rights violations would not be included in these classes....The Greens are concerned that the integrity of public education is being compromised by opportunities for a foreign government to promote views outside of the curriculum to school students. Teachers are recruited from China and paid by the Confucius Institute—an arm of the Office of Chinese Language Council International which is affiliated to the Chinese Ministry of Education. They must meet certain criteria, including not having any involvement in Falun Gong. It is clear that the teachers have been politically vetted and will be deeply prejudiced toward Beijing's orthodoxy on issues such as Tibet, Taiwan, human rights, and the Tiananmen Square massacre. The Greens welcome the teaching of Chinese language and culture, however we must be cautious of foreign government influence within our state schools. These classes are very different to other International programs such as the Alliance Francaise. Confucius classes are directly linked to and funded by the Chinese government. This is highly problematic in the teaching of language and culture, which should be free from government bias and control.

(http://nsw.greens.org.au/content/greens-mp-opposes-chinese-funded-culture-classes)

—In December 2013, the governing council of the Canadian Association of University Teachers (CAUT)—representing some 68,000 teachers in 120 colleges and universities—called upon those colleges and universities in Canada currently hosting Confucius Institutes "to cease doing so, and those contemplating such arrangements to pursue them no further." James Turk, the Executive Director of the Association, explained: "in agreeing to host Confucius Institutes, Canadian universities and colleges are compromising their own integrity by allowing the Chinese language Council International to have a voice in a number of academic matters, such as curriculum texts and topics of classroom discussion. Such interference is a fundamental violation of academic freedom." (*caut.ca*: 17 December 2013; *Anthropology Today,* February 2014).

—Following the lead of CAUT, the American Association of University Professors in June 2014 recommended that

> universities cease their involvement in Confucius Institutes unless the agreement between the university and Hanban is renegotiated so that (1) the university has unilateral control over all academic matters, including recruitment of teachers, determination of curriculum, and choice of texts; (2) the university affords Confucius Institute teachers the same academic freedom rights...that it affords all other faculty in the university; and (3) the university-Hanban agreement is made available to all members of the university community.

The AAUP objected to the supervision of Confucius Institutes by an agency of the Chinese state, itself under a member of the politburo and vice-premier of the PRC. It also found unacceptable the fact that, "Most agreements establishing Confucius Institutes feature nondisclosure clauses and unacceptable concessions to the political aims and practices of the government of China," specifically noting the advancement of a state agenda in the recruitment of academic staff, the choice of curriculum, and the restriction of debate. (http://www.aaup.org/report/partnerships-foreign-governments-case-confucius-institutes); (http://chronicle.com/article/AAUP-Rebukes-Colleges-for/147153/)

—The trustees comprising the Toronto District School Board (TDSB) agreed to open Confucius Classrooms in the district's primary and secondary schools beginning in September 2014. The Chair of the Board, Chris Bolton, who had business relations with China, had been arranging this agreement with Hanban since 2007—although the trustees would know little or nothing of the matter until 2014. Their lack of knowledge was a function of the covert way the CI was initiated--a common pattern at the university level as well (see below). According to a report in *The Globe and Mail*, Mr. Bolton simply informed the trustees at a Board meeting in May of 2012 that a formal signing ceremony with the Confucius Institutes had taken place in Ottawa the previous month. The "trustees of Canada's largest school board were never given an opportunity to vet or approve a controversial agreement with the Chinese government to offer students culture programs subsidized and controlled by Beijing." (*The Globe and Mail*: 30 June 2014) Specifically, the trustees "were not told about key aspects of the Confucius Institute, including the fact that instructors are trained to self-censor on topics that are politically taboo in China." (17 July

2014). "Perhaps Mr. Bolton thought he was getting a good deal," the paper editorialized, but in fact, "the agreement benefits a foreign government, and undermines the independence of our education system" (2 July 2014). In May 2014, when the news broke of the imminent opening of the CI in September, there was a strong protest from parents and community members, including a petition and website (saynotoci.com) initiated by a person associated with Falun Gong. Marked by a blanket and rather shrill anti-communist animus, the petition would eventually garner some 2000 signatures. Apart from the volume of complaints, however, the TDSB trustees were primarily concerned with censorship and propaganda in the classroom, and on 11 June a committee was charged with investigating such issues, the trustees to vote on their recommendations on 18 June. Mr Bolton, the Board Chair who had negotiated the CI with Hanban, precipitously resigned from the TDSB shortly before the meeting of the 18th. At that meeting, it was decided not to open the CI in September pending further investigation. The vote was overwhelming in favor of delay—although some called "on the board to sever its ties altogether with the Chinese government." Indeed, according to a later report, the Board was investigating how it could terminate the contract with Hanban.

The Hunan City University had been scheduled to provide teachers for the Toronto schools. These CI teachers would have had to pass political muster, since according to the recruitment page on the university's website, the persons recommending the applicants were required to primarily evaluate their "political thinking, teaching abilities, physical and mental health."

Comment: I am given to understand that "political thinking" or "political ideology" (zhengzhi sixiang) commonly refers to adherence to the policies and leadership of the CCP.

(*The Globe and Mail,* 17 July 2014, http://www.theglobeandmail.com/globe-debate/editorials/confucius-institute-chinese-for-conflict-of-interest/article19401054/);

(http://www.theglobeandmail.com/globe-debate/editorials/confucius-institute-chinese-for-conflict-of-interest/article19401054/);

(http://www.thestar.com/yourtoronto/education/2014/06/26/why_the_uproar_over_the_tdsbs_partnership_with_the_confucius_institute.html);

(http://www.theglobeandmail.com/news/national/education/chinese-officials-press-tdsb-not-to-abandon-confucius-institute/article19217497/);

(http://news.nationalpost.com/2014/06/18/toronto-public-school-board-delays-china-backed-confucius-institute-amid-fears-it-will-used-be-as-propaganda-tool/);

(http://www.cbc.ca/news/canada/toronto/tdsb-delays-deal-with-china-s-confucius-institute-1.2680015);

(http://classroomedition.ca/toronto-school-board-seeks-end-to-china-deal/)

—The University of Manitoba rejected the Confucius Institute. Explained Terry Russell, Professor of Asian Studies:

> We didn't see how you could reconcile inviting the Chinese government of which the Confucius Institute is basically an agent of to come on campus and present programs that wouldn't ever actually talk about human rights in China.

Or on another occasion: Russell said, "They have no particular interest in what we would call critical inquiry or academic freedom." (*Times Higher Education*: 4 April 2013; *Epoch Times*: 21 July 2011) According to another, reliable faculty source, to the extent there were faculty discussions, it was reported to the Senate that this was under consideration through our Extended Education Faculty, not the core academic faculty, but this person heard no detailed report in the Senate. Although there was some interest in a CI on the part of the Administration, "it was not welcomed more broadly, in part because it was not being supported within our small Asia Studies Centre and would not have been placed there." (personal communication) The president of the University of Manitoba Faculty Association, Cameron Morrill, also noted:

> Materials and instructors for CIs are selected and controlled by a branch of the government of the People's Republic of China...It is inappropriate to allow any government, either foreign or domestic, control over a university classroom, regardless of how much money they offer.

(http://www.insidehighered.com/news/2012/01/04/debate-over-chinese-funded-institutes-american-universities)

—From a China faculty member at the University of Kansas:

> In our case, the main thing was that the deal for the Confucius Institute came about without asking us first. I would have told the chancellor and others in the administration about my reservations about such an alliance. They did pass it by me and others after it

was already agreed to, and I was taken aback and began expressing objections, which were by then unwelcome and ineffective. I did not want an institute affiliated with a foreign government, especially this one, establishing itself inside an American academic institution and did not want it affecting or influencing our language teaching program, of which I have been a part since the 1980s. I had heard of some schools using the Confucius Institute to supply them with Chinese teachers, which in my view would take away from our professional authority to direct our program and monitor its quality. ... It also seemed to me intuitively obvious that others would share my viewpoint, but amazingly many people, including good friends in China studies here and elsewhere, have not felt the same way. So far the program exists only in a separate campus of the university (nearer to Kansas City) and mainly deals with teaching Chinese via remote learning to high schools across Kansas. I think that keeping it separate is perhaps due to the objections some of us had. We have continued to enjoy complete autonomy in our language program, and that is extremely important.

—Statement by the Chair of the Board and Director of the Confucius Institute associated with Lyon Universities 2 and 3:

The Lyon Confucius Institute (LCI) definitively ceased activities on 23rd September 2013. This situation resulted from a disagreement that had persisted since September 2012 between the Lyon-based administrators of the LCI and the HQ of Confucius Institutes in Beijing (hereafter called the Hanban). The LCI was a partnership between the Lyon 2 and Lyon 3 universities, and Sun Yat-sen University (Guangzhou).... From the very establishment of the Institute in 2009, the French side

(Lyon 2/Lyon 3), while showing enthusiasm for this partnership that Sun Yat-sen had wanted for some time, had insisted on the Institute's academic and institutional independence. In addition, for legal and deontological reasons, the Institute could not be integrated in the University itself and was not to be implicated in its teaching and research activities. In order to assure this essential separation between a French public university and an entity financed and piloted by the Chinese State, the Institute took the form of an association under the law of 1901 (in other words, a not-for-profit organization).... At the moment of its constitution, this arrangement was not contested by Beijing. Tolerated until 2012, it seemed that our institutional and intellectual independence became unacceptable to Beijing. A new director taking his instructions direct from Beijing arrived in September 2012 and questioned the content of our courses and insisted strongly on a deeper integration of the LCI in the University itself. He wanted partnerships with our research centres in the domain of sinology, and held out the promise of PhD scholarships for our students willing to pursue their studies in China, and suggested that the LCI participate in the teaching of the University degree programs. This interference in the University from an organization emanating from the Chinese state seemed to us inappropriate, since it would put in doubt our academic freedom and transgress the spirit and the regulations of the French Republic's higher education system. In hindsight, we suppose that our firm stance in not acceding to these demands explains why in November 2012, the director general of the Hanban, Madame Xu Lin, demanded the resignation of the Chair of the LCI Board and announced without warning the suspension of the Hanban's annual subsidy. Over the course of the past few months, we have tried on numerous occasions to explain that it was impossible to cede to these new and exponential demands. Supported by the LCI's Board and the President of Lyon 3 University, we have attempted for the past year to reach an understanding acceptable to both parties. Unfortunately the inflexible attitude of the Hanban has prevented all possibility of a compromise. It is with consternation that we witness the LCI experiment ending in this impasse, all the more so since we have always maintained close and fruitful relations with PRC academics and their universities.

Gregory Lee, Chair of the Board, LCI
Florent Villard, Director, LCI

—In 2007 at the University of Melbourne, the Chinese Studies Department objected to the establishment of a Confucius Institute in the Faculty of Arts; as a result it was located at a distance from the main campus and mainly devoted to outreach courses for the corporate sector.

Comment: As noted earlier, this kind of conflict with the established China program is common, as is the solution of physically displacing the CI from central campus, putting it in a branch of the university outside the core liberal arts such as the education or business school, and/or devoting it to non-credit adult courses or Confucius Classrooms.
(http://www.universityworldnews.com/articlephp? story-20071130094503100)

—Copenhagen University rejected a Confucius Institute in 2006. Recently, the Dean for Academic Research at that time, who is also a lecturer in Chinese, explained:

We very much would like to keep the university free from that sort of political interests, and especially so when the initiative comes from a state that is not democratic. We prefer to collaborate directly with Chinese academics at Chinese universities, rather than collaborate directly with a Chinese government organ.

(www.information.dk/16703000)

In another, personal communication, which also notes the rejection of a CI at Aarhus University, the dean elaborates:

It is correct that I rejected acceptance of CI at Copenhagen U and now once again at Aarhus University. There have been various Chinese attempts at various Danish institutions. But regardless what country makes such an advance my stance has been that it is unacceptable for a Danish university to open its organization for another country's educational activities in the shape of a special institute on campus. It would be OK if the activities are outside the universities, as with the British Council or the Goethe Institutes, with which universities can collaborate as they please. But organizational integration cannot be regarded as complying with the autonomy of the universities and their duty to be independent institutions of learning. We do accept lecturers sent out from other countries but these are hired as individuals and are wholly integrated in our own organization's academic life and are not part of another's (as are the staff of the CI). In addition, the many CI night school and similar activities, carried out under the aegis of its affiliations with the universities where they are located, do not accord with the university's mission to convey research knowledge.

—At Stockholm University, a medley of charges, apparently from several sources including faculty, specifiying that in various ways the CI was damaging to the academic integrity of the institution, brought about an independent investigation. The investigation was largely inconclusive; but because it documented friction between the Asian faculty and the CI teaching program, because the Chinese embassy had intervened in an internal dispute involving a CI teacher, and because the investigator judged it improper for a foreign government to be exercising pedagogical functions in the university, it was recommended that the CI be reorganized in a consortium with other universities and its Chinese teaching should be confined to adult education and other non degree courses. In response, the then Dean of Humanities said a decision had been taken to remove the CI from the university. "Simply the suspicion of influence from the Chinese state is a problem," he said, "and therefore the Confucius Institute will be an independent institute on the model of the German Goethe institutes or the Cervantes Institute." (www.information.dk/167254) Although the university president had explicitly noted this and in 2008 promised to make these changes, so far as can be determined from the Stockholm CI website, this has not happened. Commenting on the Stockholm issues, Lionel M Jensen states:

> Events of this kind offer confirmation of the criticisms of Hanban and the Confucius Institutes made by observers in Australia, Canada, India, and the United States that China's investments in cultural understanding through language and culture will compromise the candid discussion, inquiry, and research that are essential to university life.

(Jensen, op.cit., 293-94; see also Don Starr, "Chinese language Education in Europe: The Confucius Institutes," *European Journal of Education* 44: 65-83, 2009; Anders Mellbourn, "Investigative Report" [personal communication])

—The University of British Columbia has twice refused an overture to establish a Confucius Institute. The first time, of which our source, a prominent member of the Asia faculty, has no direct knowledge, was early on in the Hanban project. He does have personal knowledge of the second attempt, in 2010 as he recalls, when "the proposal, coming out of the [university] administration, was discussed and rejected by senior China and Asia faculty." The faculty, he writes, declined for two reasons: 1) that the CI added nothing substantive to the existing UBC Chinese program, which had no need for more Chinese teachers—though they could use more funding for those they have; and 2), "concerns about the tight links between Hanban and the CCP." Having been rejected by the senior Asian faculty, the proposal never got to a negotiation stage. Our source himself has "deep reservations about Confucius Institutes and their suitability for North American universities." Referring to the relevance of negotiations with Hanban elsewhere, he writes: "At the end of the day, as one colleague remarked: why spend time on making a Confucius Institute be non-toxic, when it doesn't really add to our mission?" (personal communication) A third attempt by Hanban to enlist the UBC through the forestry school is under way.

—The first CI in the US at the University of Maryland was introduced and directed by a Physics professor with ties to the PRC, but without consulting the then director of the Chinese language program (who supplied this information) or the heads of the Department, School, or College in which Chinese language and culture is taught. "The whole thing was set up in secret" through a relationship between Hanban and the Physics professor, and then between the latter and the University president. Later it was learned from the Physics professor in charge that it was arranged this way so he would not have to answer to anyone in the University but the president. Initially, most of the CI was staffed by scientists with no cogent connection to Chinese language teaching. More than one attempt was then made to have the faculty of the established Chinese language program agree to accept the CI's authority and direction for teaching Chinese, Hanban offering in return to supply the teachers, their salaries, together with the textbooks and course curricula. Writes the erstwhile head of the Chinese language program: "During my tenure at Maryland we were never willing to agree to such an obvious ploy for external manipulation" (personal communication).

Comment: In his comparative study of Confucius Institutes, Lionel M. Jensen (op. cit.) observers that a particular member of faculty is often the singular agent of the establishment of the institute. He or she will initiate the project, coach the university president on the advantages of a Confucius Institute, and act as the prime mediator with Hanban. Although not necessarily a scholar of Chinese language, history, or literature, this point person, according to Mr. Jensen, is very often ethnically Chinese or Chinese-American, and he or she could well be named the director of the institute. In this connection, Hensen notes:

> *From the vantage of a university leader the politics doesn't matter all that much. It is preferable to be meaningfully engaged in China than not.... Establishing a public mark of commitment to China and to the dissemination of Chinese language is simply very canny academic business.*

—The University of Pennsylvania rejected the Confucius Institute. The proposed establishment of a CI at Pennsylvania involved a furtive end run around the China faculty similar to the one at Maryland, based on an arrangement instead between Hanban and the Graduate School of Education. The Chinese studies faculty discovered this arrangement at the last moment, when it was about to be endorsed; whereupon their exposure of the proceedings ended them. The China scholars issued a statement explaining they did not want a program of inferior pedagogy competing with their own, one moreover that would "engage in various unwelcome soft power initiatives such as are going on everywhere there are CIs." (Lionel M. Jensen, op.cit., pp. 287-88; *Bloomberg.com*: 1 November 2011)

—At UCLA, we see the same pattern of stealth as in the establishment of a CI at Maryland and the failure thereof at Penn: "the faculty were on break and the initiative was foisted on the university with the assistance of deans and administrators." This helps explain why the CI there was set up in a wing of the university at some remove from the Asian Languages and Cultures Department—in this case again in the School of Education.

This is for a very good reason, and one that is broached in most every circumstance in which a CI initiative is proposed by Hanban with the assistance of a university administration: competition between a university's own program and that offered by Hanban is undesirable.

(Jensen, op.cit., p.288)

—Stanford followed the same pattern. The initiative for a Confucius Institute came from a faculty member of the East Asia department—a Chinese ex-pat with graduate training in the US, also a common m.o.—and was negotiated by the Dean of the School of Humanities and Sciences without broad faculty consultation or even notification of the faculty until it was an accomplished fact. (personal communication) For that matter, according to an official spokesperson, the president of the University "has not been involved in that institute or any negotiations related to it." (*Bloomberg News*: 1 November 2011) The Dean, a scholar of ancient Rome, became the Director of the Confucius Institute. He has been quoted several times in the press as being satisfied that Stanford did not compromise its academic integrity in the arrangement, nor has Hanban exerted any pressure that would have that effect—once the original suggestion that Tibet not be mentioned was rebuffed. But then, "The University plans to use [part of] the money for a professorship in classical Chinese poetry, far removed from the Tibet dispute."
Comment: No problems.

—At the University of New Hampshire, a China Committee, consisting of several high-ranking administrators and the University's two China experts, undertook the preliminary CI negotiations. After the Chinese partner institution invited the university president and his family to China, final negotiations were concluded between the administration, the university lawyer, and the Chinese partner, which eliminated a separate oversight committee. When the China Committee raised several objections, the Committee was told that its work was completed. After four years of implementation, the Faculty Senate questioned the UNH-CI terms of agreement. The faculty subsequently tabled a language minor that in effect would be controlled by the UNH-CI and the college established a committee to review the UNH-CI. (personal communication)

—At the University of Chicago, the faculty at large, including Asia scholars other than the China faculty, did not learn of the establishment of a Confucius Institute until they read about in the news. The impetus at Chicago came from a Chinese ex-pat professor, Dali Yang, with graduate training in the US and research in China. Initially, it seems that even the president, the provost, and dean presiding over the CI Board of Directors knew little about the CI. On 4 June 2010, four days after the Confucius Institute was ceremoniously opened, the president and provost had a meeting with representatives of a self-constituted faculty organization called CORES during which the CI came under discussion. CORES had organized the petition signed by 174 faculty protesting what they called the "corporatization" of the University, of which the Milton Friedman Institute and the Confucius Institute were prime examples. The minutes of this meeting were circulated to all participants and no corrections were offered to any of the contents. The contents featured the objections of two prominent East Asia scholars, Norma Field (Japan) and Bruce Cumings (Korea), to the political character of the Confucius

Institute, the role it would now play in determining what is taught about China, and how "they and other faculty members who work on East Asia had effectively been excluded from discussions and the decision-making process." They were not alone. The minutes also record that President Robert Zimmer and Provost Thomas Rosenbaum "acknowledged their lack of information on this matter and expressed bewilderment and regret at how this happened."

Although the Chicago statutes, as reaffirmed by two committee investigations, mandate faculty control of the establishment of entities with teaching responsibilities, the Council of the faculty Senate, as the appropriate "governing body," was not allowed to vote on the introduction of the CI in 2009 or its renewal in 2014. In the latter instance, a petition signed by 110 faculty members, almost all senior in rank, objecting to the presence of the Confucius Institute and calling for a Council vote on its renewal, was effectively blocked in the Council by the faculty Board of Directors of the CI and the President Robert Zimmer as presiding officer. A committee of three China scholars established and charged by the CI Board to make a report on the renewal had recommended that the teaching component be eliminated and the research component be subject to greater University control; but the recommendation was opposed in Council by the same Board of Directors (notably including a dean and ex-dean), and apparently buried. To date the report has not been seen by the faculty at large and evidently never will be. The renewal is now under consideration by the Provost—for a decision during the summer vacation.

—The adoption of a Confucius Institute at Chicago was cited as precedent for taking on a CI at George

Washington University by a GW dean; the dean said it increased their comfort level. (*GW Hatchet*: 17 January 2013)

—A member of the Asian faculty at the University of Oregon relates that he found out about the establishment of the OU Confucius Institute when he read it in the press. His letters of protest to the administration had no effect. The driving force of the arrangement was the new president of the University. "What's striking to me," he writes, "is that there was no advance warning. No public meetings. No rumors. Nothing. Orchestrated silence." (personal communication)

—In an article of 24 July 2008 in *Chinascope*, referring to Hanban under its original name (National Office for Teaching Chinese as a Foreign Language)—but speaking of its current director (Xu Lin)—it is described as

> a daily affairs organization...organized by the leaders of 11 ministries under the State Council. Its function is to coordinate the various ministries and committees to promote Chinese as a national and ethnical enterprise, going abroad in a "smooth, fine and silent" fashion.

(http://chinascope.org/main/content/view/1057/92/)

—One reason for the lack of knowledge of Confucius Institutes in the university community at large is that the agreements establishing them, ratified by one or two representatives of the host institution, are usually secret. The model agreement developed by Hanban has a nondisclosure clause—although the relevant wording is sometimes omitted, especially in contracts with prestigious universities. As published on the Hanban website, Article 14 reads (in translation from the Chinese part of the bilingual text):

> The two parties to the agreement will regard this agreement as a secret document, and without written approval from the other party, no party shall ever publicize, reveal, or make public, or allow other persons to publicize, reveal, or make public materials or information obtained or learned concerning the other party, except if publicizing, revealing, or making it public is necessary for one party to the agreement to carry out its duties under the agreement.

—Among other universities known to have rejected Confucius Institutes are the following: UC Berkeley ("rebuffed" Hanban's approach; Jensen op.cit.); Cornell (spurned invitation from Hanban, *Bloomberg News*: 1 November 2011.); Harvard ("maybe there was discussion as a broad possibility, but nothing serious," *Bloomberg News*: 1 November 2011); UC San Diego; Claremont College; Mount Holyoke; Dickinson State College; University of Sherbrooke (*The Globe and Mail*: 22 May 2011); Tokyo University; Kyoto University; The Australian National University; Southern Denmark University; Aarhus University; University of Wisconsin; University of Oslo—and they "remain very happy to have rejected it." (personal communications)

What Is To Be Done?

Reflecting on the events of July 2014 at the European Association of China Studies, where Hanban's Director General censored conference materials including academic texts not to her liking, Professor Christopher Hughes of the London School of Economics wrote: "In light of this (and what we now know about the pressure exerted on Lyon) I really do not understand those who still claim that CIs are not a political instrument of the CCP.... If they are not giving you pressure now, it is just a matter of time. The strategy is clear: establish CIs in leading universities to get credibility, spread to smaller ones on the back of that, then start to exert pressure from the small ones, combined with the carrots of the new sinology project to penetrate core activities of research and non-language teaching through the whole academic system. It really is time for academics to take a united stand on this, especially for those in more influential institutions, to support colleagues in less powerful and well endowed institutions like Lyon and in Portugal." (personal communication).

Prominent universities—Stanford, Columbia, the University of Chicago, the LSE—willing or not have functioned to legitimate the Confucius Institutes by their participation, and thereby justified and encouraged the inclinations of other institutions to do likewise. Interesting that the most esteemed universities in America, Britain, and Canada—Harvard and Yale, Oxford and Cambridge, Toronto and British Columbia—have kept clear of the CI project, ostensibly because they already have strong China programs of their own. Yet the same can be said of Chicago or

Columbia, so as the UBC professor asked, "why spend time on making a Confucius Institute be non-toxic, when it doesn't really add to our mission?" True that in the interest of enlisting the more prestigious research universities, Hanban offers more generous terms than it does for smaller colleges or municipal school districts. But unless it is holding Stanford, Columbia, and Chicago hostage for their newly constructed centers in Beijing, there seems no cogent reason for these wealthy and well-staffed universities to risk their reputations for academic freedom and integrity by subcontracting teaching and research from a Chinese government that has repeatedly shown itself to be inimical to these values. On the contrary, precisely because these great institutions are facilitating the global spread of academic and intellectual princi- ples contrary to those upon which they are founded— contrary to their own universal project of advancing human knowledge in the interest of human welfare— they ought to reverse course, terminate their relations to the Confucius Institutes, and resume their obliga- tion of living up to the idea of the university. Others will follow. ▪

Breaking News

The following important news broke just as this pamphlet was on its way to the printer:

On September 25th, four days before the contract of the University of Chicago with the Confucius Institutes of Beijing (Hanban) was scheduled to run out, the University suspended negotiations for a renewal, issuing the following statement:

> The University of Chicago has informed Madame Xu Lin, director-general of Hanban and chief executive of the Confucius Institute Headquarters, of the University's decision to suspend negotiations for the renewal of the agreement for a second term of the Confucius Institute at the University of Chicago (CIUC).
>
> Since 2009 the University of Chicago and Hanban have worked in partnership to develop the CIUC, which has benefited research on China and collaboration between the University of Chicago and academic institutions in China. The University and Hanban have engaged in several months of good faith efforts and steady progress toward a new agreement. However, recently published comments about UChicago in an article about the director-general of Hanban are incompatible with a continued equal partnership.
>
> The University is therefore suspending negotiations for the renewal of the agreement at this time. The University of Chicago remains committed to supporting the strong connections and longstanding collaborations between University of Chicago faculty and students and Chinese scholars, students, and institutions. As always, the University is guided by its core values and faculty leadership in all matters of academic importance.

The "published comments" that purportedly caused the University to suspend negotiations for a renewal of the CIUC appeared in a Chinese language online site (blog.sina.com) and were clearly intended for domestic consumption. They were near the tail of an article fulsomely praising Madame Xu Lin, Director-General of the Confucius Institute. The passage in question related how with one sentence Madame Xu was able to intimidate the president of the University of Chicago over the issue of a protest of the CIUC by members of his faculty—mistakenly described as 100 emeritus professors. The reference was to a petition to the Council of the Faculty Senate calling for termination of the University's Confucius Institute, signed by 110 professors, the great majority senior in rank and still in service.

In translation, the key part of the Chinese text read:

> Madame Xu Lin is smart, but more than that, she combines softness and toughness to a fault, and wields the combination as a weapon. Many people have tasted this. At the end of April of this year, a hundred emeritus professors at the University of Chicago in the U.S. wrote an open letter calling for an end to the university's Confucius Institute. Then Xu Lin, in a letter sent straight to the President of the University of Chicago, and in a phone call to the university's representative in Beijing, had only one sentence to say: "If you want to end the relationship, it's fine with us." Her attitude brought panic to the other side, and a quick decision that the university would continue with its Confucius Institute.

Surely the drama is not over, but as of 29th of September, 2014, the University has no contract with the Confucius Institute.

Consequently, it should receive no monies from Hanban; it should not have teachers trained, supplied and paid by Hanban offering accredited courses in its own East Asian program; it should not be required to submit research proposals of its faculty and graduate students through the CIUC for approval and funding by Beijing; and it should thus be able to restore the reputation for academic autonomy and integrity that has long distinguished it.

Also available from Prickly Paradigm Press:

continued

continued